Window to My Soul

A Collection of Poetry and Prose

By Mathew C. Goings

Window to My Soul

A Collection of Poetry and Prose

Copyright © 2024 by Mathew C. Goings

The cover art is not copyrighted and was generated using AI tools

All rights reserved.

No part of this book may be reproduced, stored in a retrieval system, or transmitted in any form or by any means—electronic, mechanical, photocopying, recording, or otherwise—without the prior written permission of the publisher, except for brief quotations used in reviews or articles.

Published by Optimistic Media LLC

ISBN: 9798305181890

Credits

Cover design by Mathew Goings using AI assistance

Legal Notices

Library of Congress Cataloging-in-Publication Data available upon request.

Printed in United States of America

First Edition: 2024

Dedication

Dedicated to my mother,

Gloria Ann Jones

The most Beautiful of Gods Creations.

My hero, and the wind beneath my wings.

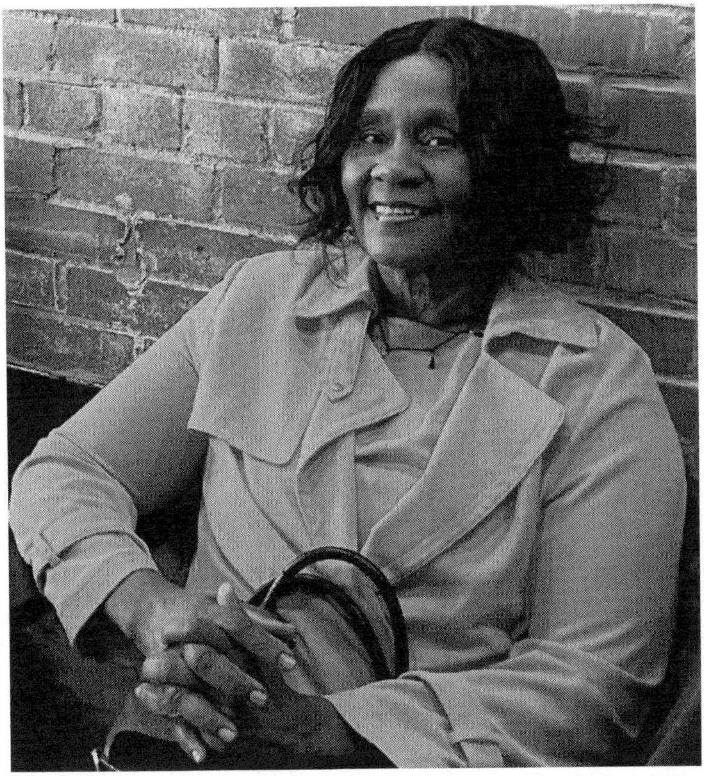

Preface

Poetry has always been my way of expressing my emotions,

and making sense of the world, -

Of capturing fleeting thoughts and feelings that otherwise slip away.

This Collection. Titled "A window to my soul" is a reflection on my journey

Through loss, healing, and growth. Each poem is a snapshot of a moment-

written over quiet nights and turbulent days of personal reflection

Over the last 3 years. As I tried to better understand myself and the world around me.

The poems ebb from darkness into light- some simply quiet observations.

While others are raw emotional outpourings.

Together they are small fragments of my own search for meaning.

I offer these poems not only as a glimpse into my soul,

But as mirror for anyone who has struggled with finding peace in uncertain times.

I hope you find something of yourself within these pages-

Whether it's a line that resonates or a poem that lingers

May these pages serve as an excellent travel companion. On your journey!

Wherever you are headed!

Contents

- **Dedication** 7
- **Preface** 9
  - **A Window to My Soul** 14
- **For the Classics** 16
  - **Sonnet #1** 17
  - **Love Since Past** 19
  - **Love Is** 21
  - **Butterflies** 23
  - **Light** 24
  - **Where Dreams Run Free** 26
  - **Free To Give** 27
  - **Fireworks** 27
  - **Not Alone** 28
  - **50/50** 28
  - **Never Stop** 29
  - **Whisper** 30
  - **Today** 31
  - **Pop Love** 32
  - **Midnight Thoughts** 33
  - **Scared** 35
  - **To Every Girl I've Ever Loved** 37

    Blessed 39
For The Mind 41
    Words 42
    Depth 43
    Non-sense 45
    My Inner Monologue 46
    Melanin 47
    Keep It Real 50
    40 51
    Between the spaces 53
    Reflection 55
    Live for Today 57
For The Family 59
    My Boys 61
    A.M.G 63
    Gloria 64
    To My Brother 65
    Trina 69
    To My Old Man 71
    Sacrifice 73
The Final Pane 75
In Closing 77

Your Turn 78

A Window to My Soul

On the pages that follow I hope you will see.

A light through a window that I know as me.

A glimpse of my heart, a piece of my soul.

Written in CAPS, *Italics* and Bold.

A bit of my truth, as seen from my eyes.

An aerial snapshot of how high my heart flies.

A few spoken words that have never been said.

Full of all the metaphors and similes,

and lucid dreams that dance through my head.

All written down for your visual pleasure

To stir both your heart and imagination to measure.

A few simple words that I hope you will treasure.

A few words I leave to linger and stay.

A gift from my heart, when I'm far away

For the Classics

The classic poets inspire the first section of this book. Shakespeare, Longfellow, Rice to name a few. Masters of language and emotion. They were able to find beauty in all things, and their words still compel us to this day. Let us take a trip together through the classic feelings of poetry we all know and love! May the words on these pages inspire your heart to love, your mind to wander, your voice to sing, your brush to stroke vivid images, may they bring you both inspiration and enlightenment.

Sonnet #1

Eternity

So many things that I wish I could say.

As clouds dispersed, the words appeared to me.

Yet spells of focus drifted far away,

A restless whisper that won't set me free.

What if this flower, severed, lost its bloom?

Its roots fast consumed in a fiery pyre?

And fear's dark shadow cast our love to gloom.

From fleeting sparks that fade and then expire.

Though fear may arise let love overcome.

And re-ignite beneath the steadfast sun.

Then lift my voice to a song from a hum.

For deep inside, I know that love has won.

Because there is you, because there is me.

Our energy transcends... Eternity!

Love Since Past

From the first very first time I looked in your eyes.

I felt this strange feeling I could never deny.

It's almost as if all truth was held in your gaze.

Revealing to me, a path through the maze.

Showing me all the world, I've not seen.

And all the many things' love can mean,

And all the strange ways love can feel,

And all the divine ways that love can heal,

And the different tears that love can cry,

And all of times love makes you wonder why.

Yet when I saw it all both future and past.

I knew this feeling would always last,

And that with you, I will always laugh.

Even then knowing we would take separate paths,

But even know I still call you friend.

I hope we both find these feelings again.

Love Is

Love is like rainbows, or the first winter snow.

Burning so bright from a single embers glow.

We call it a feeling, but I find that untrue.

I say it's our essence, the base of me, and of you.

All that we are and aspire to be.

Is made up of a love that none of us see.

It guides us each day whether we know it or not,

and even though we try love cannot be fought.

Nor can it be taught,

and when its true; It can't even be bought.

It's both internal source, and external force.

It is ebb, it is flow, yet one constant course.

It's all that I want, and all that I need,

and with every word I'll keep planting seeds.

Keep Giving love with no expectation.

And keep treating love with great adulation!

Butterflies

Butterflies never go away,

Yet they seem to never stay.

It's almost as if; eggs they lay.

Waiting for another day.

Until I hear your voice, call out and say.

That your heart too heavy weigh,

And by your side, my song should play.

In that very moment, cast out dismay.

Know that butterflies led me this way,

And on their gossamer wings we display.

All the vibrant goodness our love portray.

Light

Darkness surrounds a world untrue.

Then suddenly a dagger of light pierce through.

So bright it sears your sight at first.

So sharp it's like you've felt the worst.

Then suddenly your eyes adjust,

And you realize that you've been truly blessed.

That the light that pierced you so,

Has shown you colors never known.

Heights you never thought to reach.

and that the mountain of you,

has yet to peak.

That light it now pierces through your fear,

and you feel your goals grow ever near,

for the first time your path clear.

Like looking into the window of your soul,

and hearing the voice within you,

Your spirit is ready to overcome fear,

the rest is yours to pursue.

Where Dreams Run Free

Through flights of fancy my heart does grow.

It soars to heights some may never know.

A place so grand some can't believe,

but still so close anyone can achieve.

Where dreams break free of tethered minds,

and clouds and stars as friends align.

Floating in an ethereal state,

as if gravity bears no weight,

as if time itself has ceased,

and all the world knows only peace.

This is the place my heart shall reach,

while growing still, too, others seek.

To guide them toward the leap unseen,

to love profound and dreams serene.

Free To Give

To live is to love.

To love is to live.

These gifts I hold,

Are mine to give.

I give them to you,

With no condition.

I live to love you,

With no division.

Fireworks

The sparkle in her eyes,

Lit the fuse to his soul.

The rest... is fireworks!

Not Alone

To every moment,

Now and then.

Then and now,

In the end.

Every minute,

Everyday.

I just want to take the time to say, hey!

And let you know I see you in every way!

50/50

As his light pulled her from the darkness:

They built a home in the shade

Never Stop

Through the darkest of nights.

Through the blinding light.

Pressing ever forward,

Never knowing if it's right.

Trying to reach new heights.

The goal a fleeting flicker,

Just outside of sight.

Still, we move on, still we fight.

Until that day, we feel death's cold bite.

But not before we've burned our light.

Whisper

She whispered in his ear-

I Love You,

And no other words need he ever hear.

Today

Today I choose me,

Today I choose to be,

Brilliant, charming, full of glee.

Tomorrows joy blooms here today,

A song I'll sing along the way.

All the praise of yesterday.

My way of showing life's embrace,

Grateful for this wondrous space.

Pop Love

Our Souls are so in sync,

Every day I know that God must have spent a little more time on you.

Thinking of you I drive myself crazy, and it's tearing up my heart.

Because I just want to be with you.

I know its selfish to say bye, bye, bye to my current life,

But the two of us, can be in a better place.

I don't wanna spend one more Christmas without you!

You're the only gift I want, you're that girl, please bring it all to me.

I'm crazy for you.

Midnight Thoughts

Lying in bed awake at night.

Even in the dark, you're still in sight.

Your soul illuminates,

the path that's right.

Calling, leading, pulling tight.

To view the brightest lights.

From the highest heights.

So easily enticed,

by the brightness in your eyes.

Though only ever thinking though about your size

The size of your heart.

Of all your features it sets you apart.

Your lips like silk, your form divine,

Yet its your heart that outshines.

How hard you love eclipses the rest,

I only hope when I ask, your answer is yes.

Scared

If I told you I feared love, would you believe me?

If I told you that I'm scared to give my heart, would you see me?

Would you take a chance and take a leap?

Even knowing I've been too blind to see,

What's been standing right in front of me.

All this time you've quietly stayed,

Waiting for me to step out of the shade.

Silently watching me,

watch life pass me by.

With too much respect to try to pull me out.

Yet always standing firm and about.

Knowing that you'd guide me home,

through the dark and the doubt.

To Every Girl I've Ever Loved

To every girl I've ever loved,

In any way.

I have a few things I need to say.

Whether friends or lovers.

Still close or estranged.

Whether you're family.

Or the ones flown away.

As I put my pen to paper

Thanks, is all I can say.

You opened your hearts

And you opened your eyes.

And allowed me to see,

All the deep love inside.

All the brightness in your heart,

All the ways you care,

All the emotions I never knew were there.

Each of you, a piece of me,

Forming one grand tapestry.

Always there for me in times of need

And I hope all these words you read

Through every moment with each of you

I watched in the mirror as I grew-

To form the man, I am today.

And so again,

 Thank You! I say!

Blessed

A queen among men
A smile that makes heaven jealous
On a scale of one to ten-
 definitely 11

Sometimes I think I'm lucky
Just to gaze upon your brilliance,
You, with enough heart to care for
Millions,
And depths like the ocean
When you're lost in thought

And an air of mystique-
So rare, so profound
A presence that cannot be bought.

A connection I never knew I needed

Until one fall day when fate interceded.

And now, to know you

I truly am blessed.

Maybe in time, I'll write out the rest.

For The Mind

This next set of pages is for the mind! Poems to ignite the imagination and illuminate the dark recesses of the mind! Inspired by Plath, Whitman, Eliot, and Dickinson. These works reflect the voices of those who encouraged us to see humanity at its best while exploring the journey from life to the beyond. Existential and thought provoking, let's embark on a journey through what it means to be human- and beyond!

Words

Words are just letters all strung together.

And once they're spoken, they linger forever.

As they leave your lips you feel the quiver,

feeling the sting they're bound to deliver.

Cold chills your soul reflecting on statements made.

With a feeling inside this mistake may have been grave,

and heavy a heart, the damage is made.

Depth

When your thoughts are a jumble,

and lost in fears lair.

You can't tell if these thoughts are yours to bear,

Or planted by forces beyond your care.

And things people say you're not sure if they mean

And you doubt yourself, and doubt in your dreams,

and you doubt that anyone on the outside can see,

The fine cracks that splinter deep down to your soul.

and all the pressure has taken its toll.

Casting a shadow every time you feel hope.

Emotions so real you only pretend to cope.

Because deep inside just where would you start?

Building a foundation out of the dark.

With just a spark, you find your way,

A quiet light to guide the fray.

Through cracks and shadows, you learn to see.

That even in darkness your light sets you free.

Non-sense

In a world where nothing makes sense.

Non-sense in essence, is the best sense.

As laughter brings hope to the hopeless,

joy can bring rest to the restless,

And it has since adolescence, hence.

Take time to thank those blessed with the gift of nonsense.

Since everyday they make the world a little less tense!

My Inner Monologue

Quizzes, quandaries, and quagmires abound.

On a quintessential quest to be first in queue.

Avoiding quaking quadrants quick to quell my spirit.

With no qualms, my qubits quicken through our quantum world,

Seeking to quench a dream that's quixotic and bright

Quietly I quest through the qualifiers snare,

only to quaere, does the road end or does it disappear.

Melanin

Golden, tan, brown,

Caramel, mocha, chocolate.

All different shades of a rainbow,

History would have you forget.

But the melanin you see,

Comes from a place you cannot!

Through bloodlines sold, and bloodlines bought,

Scattered out through many lands.

Worked and traded, passed hand to hand,

Reduced to nothing,

Child, woman or man,

So, the melanin you see.

Comes from a place you cannot!

An everyday semblance of all those that fought!

For their future- for our future.

Through prosecution and trials.

Not soon forgot.

Hands that crawled so we could stand tall,

Voices silenced to give speech to all.

So, the melanin you see.

Comes from a place you cannot!

A place of stories, of strength, and of might-

A legacy that still burns bright.

Keep It Real

Tell me your Tale, and I'll tell you mine

Need not be told in rhythm and rhyme

Just words of truth

Both bitter and bold

Or kind and caring, so long as it's told

Deep underneath, without bitten tongue

Just the purest of facts, telling me how you feel

In other words, friend just keep it real.

40

When I was 8, I knew no hate.

When I was 8, my life was great.

When I was 8, new friends came daily.

When I was 8, It was all yes's and maybe's.

Even though I was 8, I was really, just a baby.

Then at 10 the world began to set in

When I was 10, I rode bikes with friends

Just across town, but it felt like the world

Since I was 10, I really liked girls

And If I could go back, I'd be 10 again

And then in a Flash 20 years had passed

The young and fun days that I thought would last

Another 20 flew, and life turned a page,

Watching my children grow through each stage.

Now here I stand like I'm 40 feet tall

Though really that's the number of years through it all

The number of winters, springs, summers, and falls.

Oh, how I look forward to so many more

I'll write it again in another 2 score.

Between the spaces

Even though I'm always smiling.

I feel like I'm one breath from drowning.

The pressure bears down consuming my soul,

Yet they say it is needed to make diamond from coals.

Still wondering if I have what it takes,

And who I'd let down if I were to break.

Wondering who at the end will still be,

If I should say fuck it and do it for me.

Does anything I do truly make a difference.

If I let it go now, could I still make it different.

In the crossfire, those hurt are the innocent.

It's eminent, the denizens, say it was never meant to be a problem,

then they go and ponder how to solve them.

Never understanding that it's not about them.

The issue is time, as it goes, we grow, some fast and some slow.

Time moves onward; we grow, some fast, some slow.

Widening the space, leaving us to wonder where to go.

Reflection

It's 6:30 in the morning and what do I see.

A reflection in the mirror that's no longer me.

Or maybe it is, maybe I forgot who the real me is.

So, I reach out to shake my own hand,

The mirror reaches back, my hand held still.

Filling it with sand, my memories spill.

Holding a vision of every version of me

Like a roller coaster ride through my history.

My mirrored lips move but the words are a mystery.

What is it that I'm trying to tell myself?

Is it to remember who I am and who I'm meant to be.

That no matter how I try I cannot dim the light in me.

To illuminate the world instead of trying to keep it privately.

I think that I'm saying all the above.

Reminding myself to show self-love,
because that's the best love.

Pour out my heart in poetry and rhymes like Quest Love.

Now I hear my reflection telling me no stress, love.

Each day rise and try to give love,

And let the rest drift, like the clouds above.

Live for Today

I live for today, but with tomorrow in mind,

Though it may never come, I'll not fall behind.

I won't let tomorrow interfere with today,

I plan to have it tomorrow- needless to say.

So, I live for today but with tomorrow in mind.

And for today, I try to find

The Joy in sorrow, the pleasure in pain,

The light through the darkness that remains.

I can't go through life, living half-blind,

So, I live for today with tomorrow in mind.

Embrace every feeling- the wind and the rain,

The smell of the lilacs, the noise of a plane.

The laughter of children still sounds the same,

Like the song of a bird who has no name

Keep seeking wonder, and wonder you'll find

So, I live for today with tomorrow in mind.

.

For The Family

These final pages are a style all my own. The inspiration comes from my mother, children, siblings, and all the friends I consider family. They have shed light on my path. Brightened my days, and nights, and truly helped shape the man I am today.

This is the first time I have put many of these thoughts and emotions into words, so I present them to you, as a gift- a heartfelt reminder of those we hold close.

My Boys

The light of my life,

The Joy in my world.

Everything I do, every day is for you

I know sometimes, it doesn't seem to be true.

Being a part of your life is all I've ever wanted to do.

From your first steps to your first throw.

A joy so pure, I hope one day you'll know.

To plant some seeds, and watch them bloom

Through sunny days and rainy gloom.

To play in leaves and snow and sun,

And see the young men that you've become.

Each fleeting, moment cherished, every one.

Until the day someone calls you beau

Or boo, or bae that's the one they say today!

Soon you'll be grown and off to find your own way,

But before that I just want to say.

I love you for who you are, unconditionally, and every day!

A.M.G

20 years have come and gone

Since I've seen your face

I sit and wonder where you've found your place.

In this vast world that bends to your grace.

Is it your strength, your wit, your radiant heart.

That's made you thrive while we're apart

Just four short years of laughter and tears

Memories etched that defy years.

My one regret is not making more

Not seeing all the moments

Your life had in store

I loved you then, I love you now, I'll love you ever more!

Gloria

What could such a wonderful name mean?

Generous, Loving, Original, Radiant, Intelligent, Admirable.

Or maybe it's?

Gentle, Loyal, Open, Reliable, Independent, Astonishing.

No, it must be.

Graceful, Lively, Optimistic, Real, Incredible, Amiable

Some say it means

Immortal Glory

A name to echo through history.

But to me, it means warmth, a guiding calm,

For Gloria, to me, just means Mom.

To My Brother

It's been 20 years and what can I say?

In my mind it still feels like yesterday.

A Big package came with a brand-new video game,

And on the from line there was your Name.

Just one day later there came a change.

The phone call came in,

Our mom burst into tears.

Because that's the night she

Confirmed her worst fears.

They said you were gone!

Gunned down in the street.

On the way to send gifts.

To Colorado Springs.

I watched her heart shatter.

As she fell to the floor.

Knowing her firstborn/ will never be at her door.

I was so small I didn't know what to do

So, I dropped to the floor and began to cry too.

We sat and we spoke about you.

I may have been young, but I still had a few.

Still to this day,

those tears haven't dried

Every year on your birthday she sits

And she tries.

To let the time pass,

And with it the pain.

Passing by your picture she has in a frame.

But since you've been gone

It isn't the same.

I know one day we'll see you again.

And on that day forever begins.

Until that day know that we carry you with us-

In every memory

In every moment you should have been here.

Trina

Sunday afternoon we had a glass of wine

Then on Thursday morning I guess it was your time

I never saw it coming, I might as well be blind

Mom called and said you had passed

"Passed out" I thought inside and laughed.

But passed on is what she said

I had to let that play twice inside my head.

Making sure I heard her right.

"But she was just here the other night

How could she be gone?

It hasn't been that long?

Standing there in disbelief.

Trying to offer my mom relief.

I realized right then what you meant to me.

I remember a short time back in 1989.

When it was just us two.

Fresh off a bus in a brand-new city

I Never thought about a time

you wouldn't be here with me

Now cassette tapes, Fila shoes,

Potato chips and hot sauce all remind me of you.

I saw your whole life flash.

Like I had died too.

I guess, I mean, What I'm trying to say.

Is that you're missed here every day.

But we live on and celebrate you.

In every way.

To My Old Man

We've had our ups

We've had our downs

We've had some crazy all around

Like running you all over town

When I was young, you "I can't stand"

Now as a man I think I finally understand

You did what you could

With the cards you were dealt

I don't even think I considered how you felt

Or where you're from as a contributing factor

I just thought you were a terrible actor

To set an example, you need an example

And that was something you never had

Now I too know the struggles of being a dad

Even as I write this our time draws near an end

So now it's time to put emotion to pen

So here are a few words just between men

I love you, old man

And need you to hear it

And no, I don't forgive you

No forgiveness is needed

If things had been different

Who knows where I would be

I wouldn't have the blessings I have in front of me

My children may not have grown so beautifully

So here is a Thanks

To you from me.

Sacrifice

I watched my mom sacrifice so many things.

I was a kid I didn't know what it means.

To give up her pleasure and struggle through pain.

That's Sacrifice.

Her only driven goal,

To simply maintain.

A roof over our heads.

And food on our plates.

Going to work early,

And getting off late!

That's Sacrifice.

Always teaching love,

And never preaching hate!

Finding time to play a game,

And treating all humans the same!

Now that I'm older,

With kids of my own.

All I can do is praise her for doing it alone.

Keeping the pace and setting the tone.

Mapping out the blueprint that I use today.

To help show my sons a new kind of way.

Blessed every day, by the sacrifice you made.

The Final Pane

Staring out into the rain, looking through the final pane.

All the others too fogged to see,

decorated with "smiley faces" and "clean me".

Yet there's this one that's clear as can be.

While I peer out over the ocean I know as my soul,

 Emotions crashing like waves, I realize this world can be cold.

And often those too bold

leave others jaded with truth often left unstated.

And though many say to live is pain.

I still have this one clear pane.

 Maybe not clear but just a tint of rose,

that reminds now to take things slow.

To find the beauty and continue to grow.

To hold my head high, but not forget those who feel low.

To always smile because it will always show.

That's what I see through the final pane,

and that's what I'll share with all those in range.

A final view- soft, clear, and true.

In Closing

Thank you, for taking the time to sit and peer through the Window to My Soul! I hope this experience leaves you feeling. Feeling loved, inspired, and motivated to succeed. this is the first of my collections, but certainly not the last. With each new collection, I aim to leave you with a sense of completeness. I look forward to sharing many more beautiful journeys with you through the world of poetry. The pages following are left blank with purpose, please use them to write notes, favorite lines, comments to help you remember the value that you found in these passages.

Your Turn

The next few pages are left blank for you to fill in.

Made in the USA
Columbia, SC
31 January 2025